INSECTS

Photo-Fact Collection

Scientific Consultant
Jennifer Gresham
Director of Education
Zoo New England

Kidsbooks®

3535 West Peterson Avenue
Chicago, IL 60659

Printed in China
101301001SZ

Visit us at **www.kidsbooks.com**

Ladybug

CONTENTS

The Wonder of Insects

We live in a world of insects. Close to one million different species have been identified, making them the most abundant group of creatures on Earth. From flies and bees to butterflies, ants, and beetles, insects are found all over the world. One acre of ground may be home to more than a million insects!

Shapes & Sizes

Some insects are so tiny that you need a magnifying glass or microscope to get a good look at them. Unmagnified, the flea (right) is just one-sixteenth of an inch long. Other insects are huge—as big as a bird!

Elephant beetle

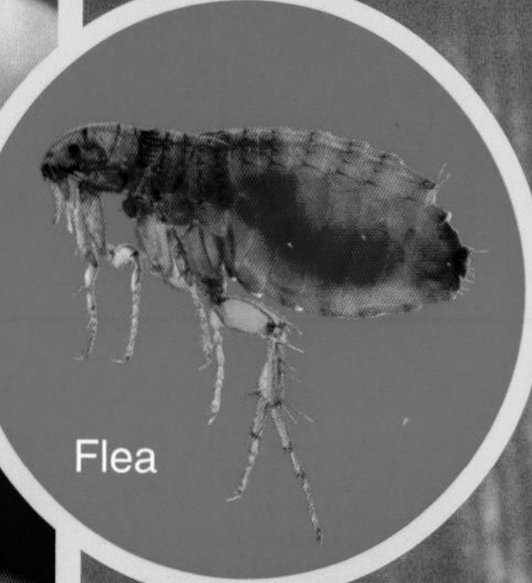

Flea

Monarch caterpillar

All Over the World

Insects live everywhere: at the frozen North and South Poles and in blazing-hot deserts, in rivers and lakes, in rain forests and farm fields—even in the biggest cities. Tropical areas are home to many of the largest beetles, butterflies, and ants.

Scarab beetle

Ancient Insects

Insects have been on Earth for more than 300 million years—since before the days of the dinosaurs. We have found insect fossils (like these trapped in amber) from long ago. Insects were the first creatures to develop wings and fly, which helped them escape from predators and find new places to live.

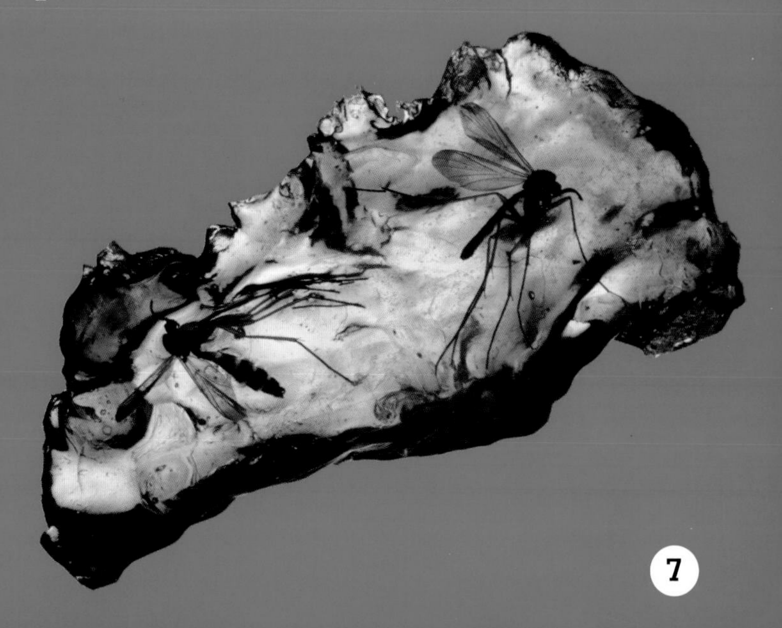

Pollinators

Lots of plants reproduce by making flowers—but the flowers can't make seeds until they get pollinated. Bees, butterflies, moths, and some beetles are pollinators: when they visit a flower to eat, they get covered in pollen, a soft powdery substance. They spread it as they go from flower to flower.

Honeybee

Recyclers

Carrion beetles feed on yucky stuff, such as dead animals, fur, and feathers. They help prevent the spread of disease by turning waste materials into fresh new soil that is rich in nutrients. This helps plants grow, making food for other animals.

Carrion beetle

Bat Food

Insects are also food for many of the bats of the Northern hemisphere. A little brown bat can eat thousands of insects, like mosquitoes, in one night.

Insects in the Web of Life

Only one percent of all insects are the pesky kind that causes problems. What do all the others do? In nature, all living things are part of the food chain. Insects are a major source of food for millions of different animal species. They do other important work, too.

Count to Six

Look at any kind of insect—a beetle, a butterfly, a termite—and you'll see six legs. Spiders, which have eight legs, are not insects (although they are related). Centipedes and millipedes look pretty buggy, too, but they have lots of legs—far too many to be insects.

Beetle

Millipede

Up for Grabs

The mouth of an insect is adapted to whatever that species eats—whether it chews leaves, sweeps the water for microscopic plants and animals, grabs and cuts into large prey, or bores into the tough wood of trees.

longhorn beetle

Insect Equipment

What makes an insect an insect? How can you distinguish insects from other creepy crawlies? It's not so hard. All of the world's insects have a few things in common. Insects have three body parts, six legs, and antennae, but not all have wings.

longhorn beetle

Major Body Parts

Most adult insects have three major body parts: head, thorax, and abdomen. The head includes the eyes, antennae, and mouth. The thorax, which separates the head from the abdomen, is where the insect's wings and legs are attached. The abdomen is the largest part. It houses the insect's heart, digestive system, and tubes for breathing.

A Bug's Life

A baby insect doesn't look much like it will as an adult. It goes through a number of big changes in its lifetime. This process of transformation is called *metamorphosis,* a word that means *a great change in body or appearance*.

Hawkmoth caterpillar

An Egg Start

All insects begin as eggs. Females lay eggs in a sheltered place, such as under the ground, in the bark of a tree, or at the bottom of a stream.

Shield bug eggs and babies

Incomplete Metamorphosis

Dragonflies, cockroaches, grasshoppers, and stoneflies become adults through incomplete metamorphosis. The young, called nymphs, molt (shed their skin) many times, growing steadily larger and more like adults. For its final molt, this dragonfly nymph found a rock or a branch. Its skin split open, and the adult flew off.

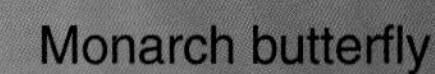

Monarch butterfly

Complete Metamorphosis

A caterpillar makes a J shape (1). It turns into a pupa (2). Protected by a tough outer case called a chrysalis (3). The pupa forms legs, wings, and a new body. It starts to emerge (4), begins drying its wings (5), floods lymph into its wings to make them full (6) and is finally a full adult monarch butterfly (7). The butterfly looks very different from its younger self!

Butterflies & Moths

With their awesome colors, shapes, and sizes, butterflies and moths are some of the coolest insects around. You know that it's summer when you see them floating over flower gardens, ponds, and fields.

Butterflies

Moth or Butterfly?

How can you tell a moth from a butterfly? Moth antennae are lined with feathery hairs and have no club at the end; butterfly antennae have a small knob at the end. Moths rest with their wings out flat or angled like a tent; when butterflies rest, they fold their wings straight up.

Luna moth

Super Sippers

Adult moths and butterflies don't eat—they drink. They have a flexible, hollow tube, called a proboscis, for a mouth. They extend the proboscis into a flower's blossom, find the nectar, and drink it up, the way you use a straw.

Butterfly

What's in a Wing?

Butterfly and moth wings are made of tiny scales that overlap like shingles on a house. Some scales contain pigments that give moths and butterflies their incredible colors.

Bark? Twig? Bug!

When this leaf insect stops moving, it looks like a leaf, blending with its surroundings. Moths and butterflies have wing colors that match the leaves or bark of trees—even the shapes of some leaves! When they sit still, birds, rodents, and other predators can't see them.

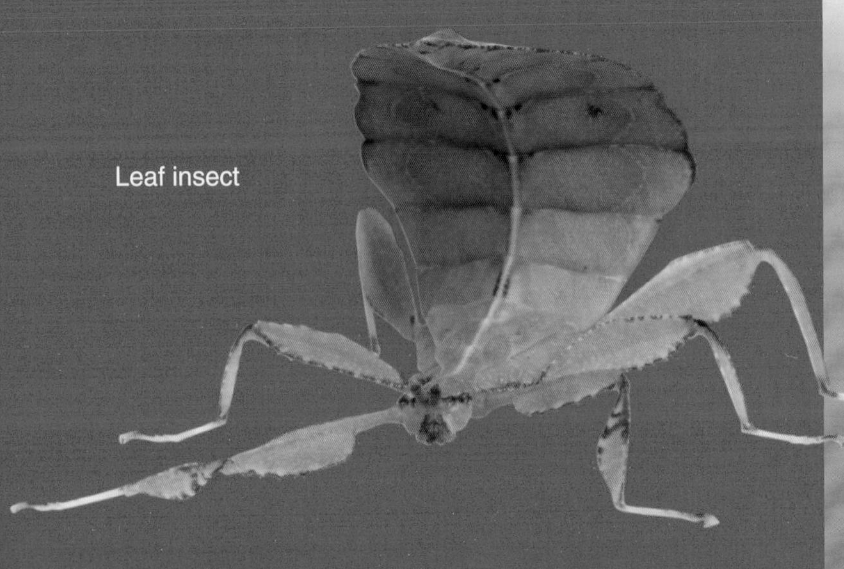

Leaf insect

Row, Row, Row

Water striders stay afloat on long legs coated with waxy, waterproof hairs, and use their middle legs like oars to move across water. They live on ponds, rivers, or oceans, eating insects they find on the water's surface. (They eat each other, too!) They inject their prey with an enzyme that turns its head into mush.

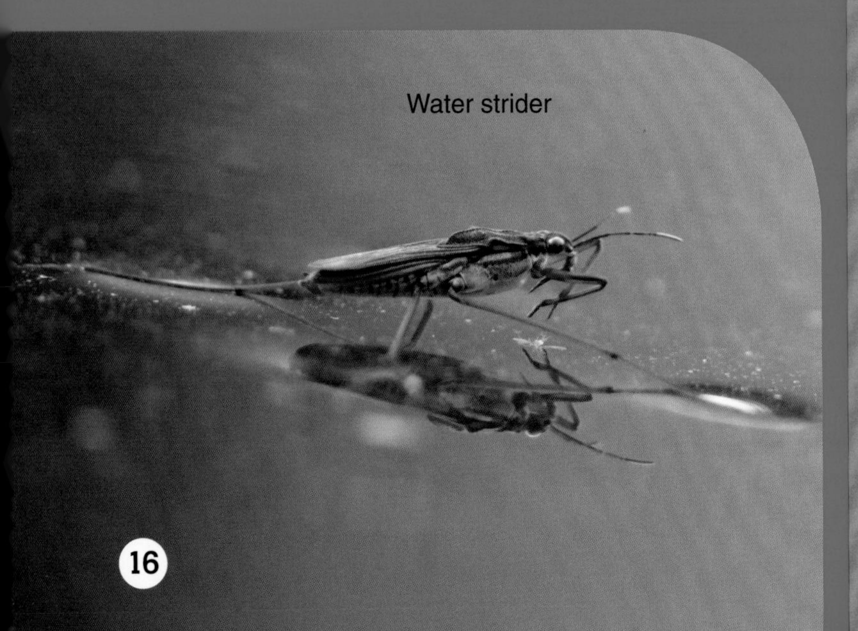

Water strider

Orchid mantis

Hunters & Hunted

Every single day, an insect must find enough food while making sure that other animals don't feed on it! But insects have been playing this game for millions of years, and have developed a lot of tricks to help them survive. The orchid mantis resembles a flower, luring other insects and small lizards into its clutches.

Speed Demon

The dragonfly is the fastest flier and has the keenest vision of any insect. It can see in almost every direction at once, and keeps its huge eyes clean by using special brushes on its front legs. Zooming after mayflies, mosquitoes, and other small insects, a dragonfly can hit 60 miles per hour! Male dragonflies establish territories and will dive-bomb other males that get too close.

Dragonfly

Seeing, Hearing, Smelling

Nearly all insects have eyes and ears. Though seeing and hearing are useful, taste and smell are an insect's most important senses. Insects taste and smell the air, ground, and leaves and flowers of plants in order to determine what is and is not safe to eat.

Grasshopper

I Hear You Calling

Hearing is all-important for katydids and bush crickets. There are more than 100 types of katydids in North America and each kind has its own song, made by rubbing its wings together. Usually, only the males sing. They sing when it's time to mate, to help females find them.

Bush cricket

Show Me the Way

Fireflies are beetles, not flies. On late summer evenings, firefly males and females put on a show as they locate one another for mating. The male goes first: he sends out a pattern of flashes as he flies, then waits for a female to reply. Special cells in the firefly's abdomen produce the light.

Lightning beetle

A Bug's-Eye View

Most insects have two large compound eyes, plus three smaller, simple eyes on top of their head. The compound eyes contain hundreds of individual eyes, called facets. Each facet gives the insects a separate picture of the world. You can see the many facets in this fly's eyes.

Meet the Beetles

With about 300,000 species known today, beetles make up one-fourth of all the world's animal life! Beetles have super-tough exoskeletons; they can fly and dig burrows; some can swim. Their colors, sizes, and mouths are adapted to where they live.

Fold-Up Wings

Most insects have four wings, but beetle wings are different. Instead of being light and flexible, a beetle's front wings are hard, almost like a shell. At rest, the hard wings—called elytra (ELL-uh-truh)—fold tightly over the other set of wings like a cover. When the beetle gets ready to fly, the elytra open so the flying wings can unfold and swing out.

Ladybug

Rainbow shield bug

Giraffe weevil

Weevils Rule!

Weevils are the largest family of beetle and the most abundant beetle, with more than 50,000 species. You can pick out a weevil easily: it has a long snout used for boring into plant stems. On the snout's tip is a pair of jaws. The weevil's antennae grow out of its snout.

Dung beetles

Clean-Up Crew

The world would be a lot smellier without dung beetles! They consume huge amounts of dung–droppings from cows, buffalo, elephants, and other animals. Some females roll it into a tightly packed ball and then lay their eggs in it.

HORNS AND JAWS

Rhinoceros beetles

Some male beetles have enormous jaws and horns. When it's time to defend their territory or battle for a mate, these fellows get mean, pushing and jousting. The fight usually ends when one beetle gets knocked to the ground from a tree limb or log.

Shake It!

Social insects need to know many things, such as where food is and whether danger is near. Honeybees perform a "dance" to let other worker bees know where nectar is. The dance provides important information—such as direction, distance, and quantity of the nectar source.

Papier-Mâché

A single paper-wasp queen starts a new colony each year. She chews up softened wood to make a soft, papier-mâché–like material for the nest. She lays eggs and raises the first worker wasps on her own. Then the workers, all females, take over. On hot days, they cool the nest by fanning their wings, or collecting water to spread over eggs and the larvae.

Social Insects

Most insects live on their own, coming together only when it's time to mate. But ants, honeybees, some wasps and hornets, and termites are social insects. They build large colonies, and each member has a job to do.

Honeybees

High-Rise Homes

Compass termites live in Australia. They build huge, wedge-shaped mounds using soil and their own sticky secretions. Some of these towers stand 15 feet or higher and are almost waterproof. The narrow ends at the top of each mound always face north and south. If you're lost in the Australian outback, find one of these mounds and use it like a compass!

Euonymus caterpillars

Helpful & Harmful Insects

There are many kinds of helpful insects. Bees produce honey and wax, mantids eat garden pests, and—for some people—insects make a nutritious, good-tasting meal! There are bad-guy bugs, too: a few kinds that make plenty of trouble for humans. It's never easy to stop them, but we keep trying!

May I Help You?

Praying mantises help us out by doing what comes naturally—eating other bugs. The ones they like to eat are usually the same kinds that wreck crops and gardens. (They also enjoy a tasty lizard or frog now and then!)

Praying mantis

Buzzzz

There are more than 2,500 kinds of mosquitoes. Male mosquitoes eat nectar; only females drink blood. Their bite can spread such fatal diseases as malaria and yellow fever to humans. But they provide food for lots of other animals so they aren't all bad!

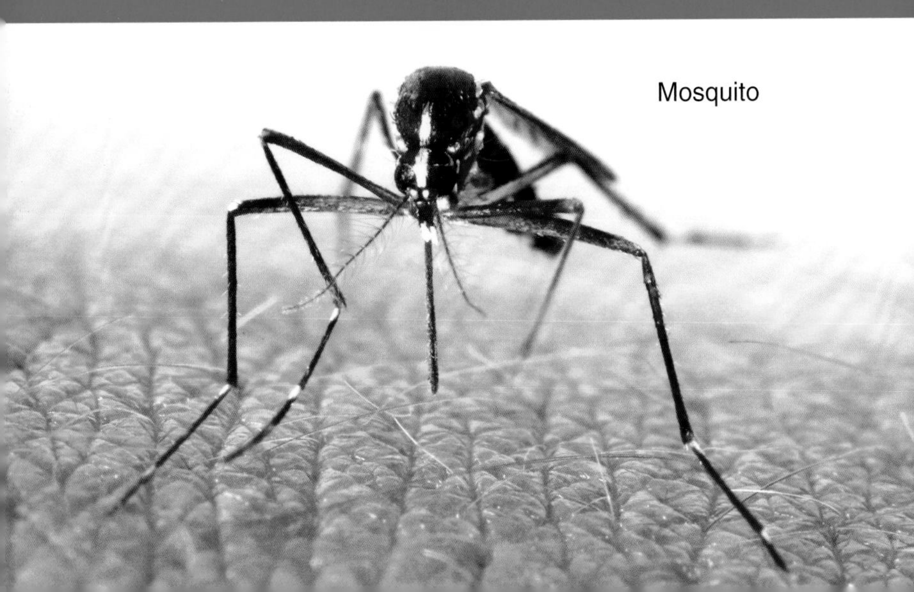
Mosquito

Grasshoppers

TIMBER!

Many kinds of insects—including grasshoppers, beetles, and moths—eat the bark, leaves, and wood of trees. Grasshoppers are defoliators, which means that they eat a plant leaves, not bark or wood.

"Killer bees" are really African honeybees. Beekeepers brought them to Brazil—then they escaped, breeding with other bees as they moved north. African bees are quick to defend their hives, but rarely attack people. Africanized bees make great honey.

They're Everywhere

The cabbage butterfly is now so plentiful in the U.S. that it's hard to believe it's a relative newcomer. A native of England, it somehow got to Canada, where it took wing and spread throughout North America.

Insects Get Around!

Insects are always looking for new places to live. They get into clothes and food shipments, airplanes and boats, luggage and boxes. Wherever people go, insects go, too. There is no way to stop them.

Ant

City Pest

American cockroaches, which are really from Africa and were introduced to the United States, have been around for 280 million years. They are so tough that one can live for nearly three days without its head! Cockroaches live by the millions in urban areas, feeding on food scraps and other debris. They are very fast and can squeeze into the smallest spaces.

A Balancing Act

The natural world is one big balancing act—and insects are a vital part of it. Studying insects is a great way to learn about nature, because insects are easy to find. Be like an entomologist: all you need is a field guide and a magnifying glass. Just make sure you don't keep the insects you find for more than a few minutes so that they can survive.

Come and Get It

If you really like butterflies and want to watch them, ask a parent or caregiver about planting a butterfly garden. There are certain types of flowers that butterflies can't resist—ask about them at a garden store. Plant a few and then see how many kinds of butterflies visit.

European peacock butterfly

Our Changing World

Many insects have adapted to one kind of habitat (natural home). People need homes, too, so every year a little more of the world's rain forests are cleared away. Birds, insects, and other rain forest animals become extinct—and we lose some of what helps to preserve a delicate balance.

Keeping the Balance

Why care about insects—yellow jackets like these, for instance? Without these wasps to eat caterpillars, we might not have some of our favorite flowers, because the caterpillars would destroy them. We need many different kinds of plants and animals to keep nature in balance.

GLOSSARY

Amber: A hard, yellowish, see-through substance made of fossilized tree resin.

Antennae: Segmented sense organs, attached to an insect's head that help it smell and touch.

Carrion: The rotting flesh of a dead animal. (Carrion beetles feed on dead animals, fur, and feathers.)

Chrysalis: The hardened shell that a caterpillar creates around itself as it attaches itself to a tree limb or other structure and begins the process of metamorphosis (transformation) into a butterfly.

Cocoon: The protective covering spun by the larva of an insect before it undergoes metamorphosis, or transformation, into its adult form.

Defoliator: Insects, such as certain caterpillars, that eat a tree's leaves but not its bark or wood.

Elytra: The hard front wings of a beetle. The elytra fold tightly over the other set of wings like a cover.

Entomologist: Scientist who studies insects.

Exoskeleton: A hard, outer skeleton or shell that protects an insect's fragile internal organs.

Facets: The hundreds of eyes contained in the compound eyes of an insect.

Fossil: The remains or impression of an animal or plant naturally preserved in rock or other hard substances.

Fungus: Any member of the group of organisms called fungi, such as mold, rust, and mushrooms.

Habitat: The area where an animal or plant naturally lives or grows.

Invertebrates: Animals that do not have backbones – such as insects, spiders, and earthworms.

Larva: A hatchling insect that does not look like its parents. After feeding and growing, larvae metamorphose into adult forms that do resemble their parents.

Metamorphosis: The changes in form during the life of an animal. Larvae, such as caterpillars, metamorphose into butterflies or moths.

Nectar: The sweet liquid of certain plants, used to make honey.

Nymph: A young insect that becomes adult through incomplete metamorphosis, molting many times until it resembles its parents.

Pollination: The process of fertilizing a plant. Bees, butterflies, moths, and some beetles pollinate flowers by spreading pollen from flower to flower.

Predator: An animal that hunts other animals for food.

Proboscis: The flexible, hollow tube that serves as a butterfly's mouth.

Pupa: The stage between larva and adult of a metamorphic insect, when legs, wings, and a new body are formed.

Serrated: Having a notched edge, like a saw or a steak knife. (The serrated front legs of the praying mantis give it extra gripping power.)

Species: A group of animals that mate and produce offspring with each other but do not breed with animals of another group; an animal belonging to a biological classification.

Thorax: The middle of the three sections of an insect's body, where wings and legs are located.